ALL ABOUT
Grizzly Bears

WRITTEN BY
Jordan Hoffman

Grizzly bears are mammals. Caribou, bowhead whales, and humans are other types of mammals.

Grizzly bears belong to the same family as polar bears and black bears. Grizzly bears are sometimes called brown bears.

grizzly bear

Polar bears are the largest species of bear on Earth, and grizzly bears are the next largest. Grizzly bears grow to an average length of 2.6 metres.

polar bear

Adult females weigh between 120 and 160 kilograms. Adult males usually weigh between 150 and 250 kilograms, but can weigh up to 380 kilograms. That is heavier than a snowmobile!

Grizzly bears found in Nunavut are usually smaller than those found in southern Canada.

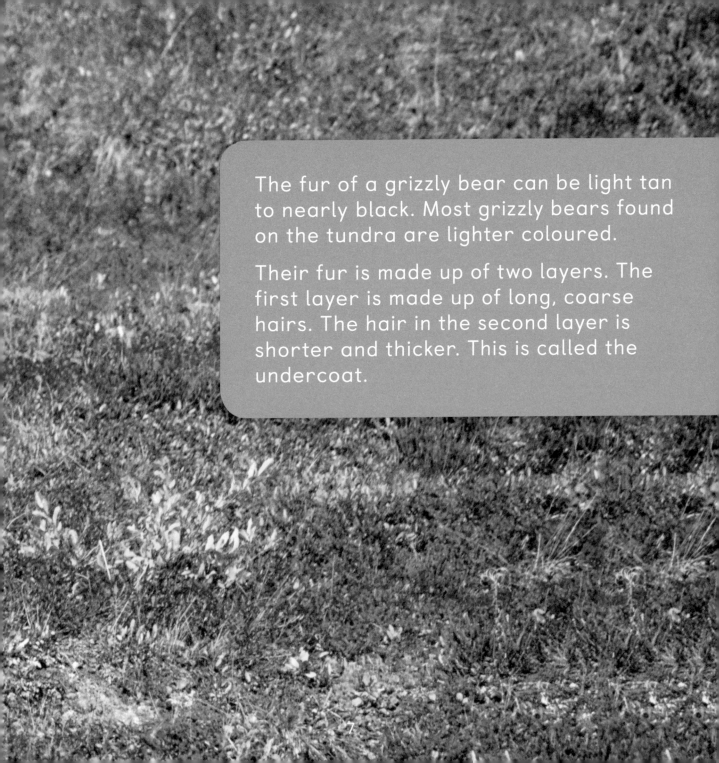

The fur of a grizzly bear can be light tan to nearly black. Most grizzly bears found on the tundra are lighter coloured.

Their fur is made up of two layers. The first layer is made up of long, coarse hairs. The hair in the second layer is shorter and thicker. This is called the undercoat.

Grizzly bears have a large hump on their shoulders. One way you can tell a grizzly bear apart from a black bear in southern Canada is by their shoulders. Black bears do not have a hump on their shoulders.

Grizzly bears have large heads with a long snout. They have two small ears with lots of fur on them. They also have long claws on their front feet.

Grizzly bears look different in the autumn than they do in the spring.

In spring, grizzly bears are skinnier. Their coats also become shorter for the warm summer ahead.

In autumn, grizzly bears are fatter. They also grow long, shaggy coats for the cold winter.

Grizzly bears live in some parts of Nunavut. They can be found on the tundra. They can sometimes be found close to communities as they search for food.

Grizzly bears can travel long distances. Males usually travel much farther than females.

Cambridge Bay

Kugluktuk

Baker Lake

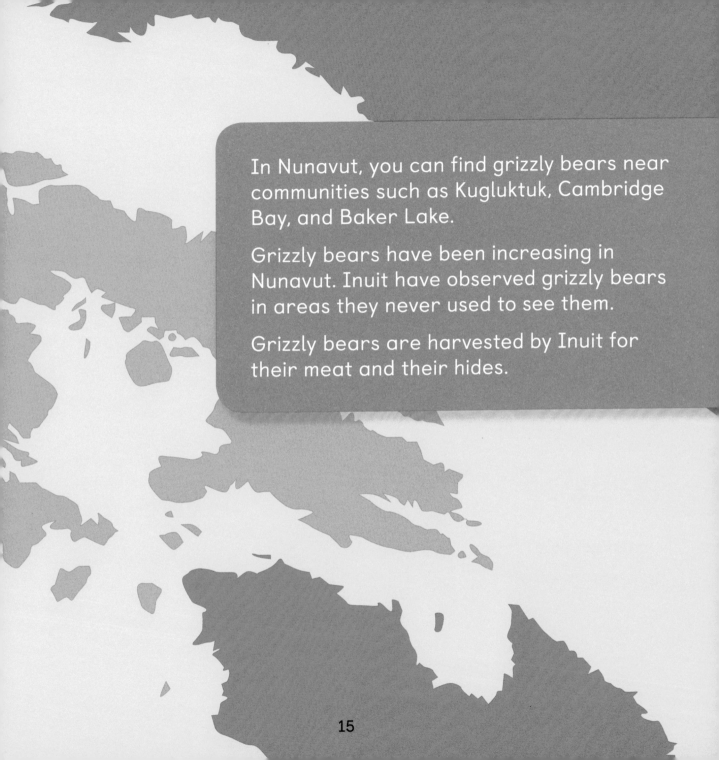

In Nunavut, you can find grizzly bears near communities such as Kugluktuk, Cambridge Bay, and Baker Lake.

Grizzly bears have been increasing in Nunavut. Inuit have observed grizzly bears in areas they never used to see them.

Grizzly bears are harvested by Inuit for their meat and their hides.

Grizzly bears are **omnivores**. They eat many different types of animals and plants.

In some areas, caribou are an important food source for grizzly bears. Grizzly bears also feed on smaller animals, such as lemmings, siksiks, and ptarmigans.

lemming

ptarmigan

An **omnivore** is an animal that eats both plants and other animals.

Grizzly bears eat plants such as Arctic cotton, blueberries, and crowberries in the summer.

Arctic cotton

crowberries

A **den** is a shelter made by animals such as bears to stay warm and protected from the winter weather. In Nunavut, they are usually under tall shrubs and are covered in snow.

Grizzly bears usually enter their **dens** in the last two weeks of October. Grizzly bears spend the long, cold winters in their dens. Males usually leave their dens in late April, while females usually leave in early May.

The young of grizzly bears are called cubs.

Female grizzly bears give birth for the first time when they are between six and eight years old. Females can have up to four cubs at one time, but they usually have two cubs.

Grizzly bear cubs are born in a den in January and leave the den with their mother in early May. Cubs stay with their mother until they are about two years old.

Grizzly bears are one of the many amazing animals found in Nunavut.

There are between 1500 and 2000 grizzly bears living in Nunavut! Have you ever seen a grizzly bear on the land?

Nunavummi